NATIONALITIES, NATIONS, AND IMPERIALIST GLOBALISATION

JAMES CONNOLLY MEMORIAL LECTURE, 2012

ROBERT GRIFFITHS

GENERAL SECRETARY, COMMUNIST PARTY OF BRITAIN

DUBLIN: COMMUNIST PARTY OF IRELAND
LONDON: COMMUNIST PARTY OF BRITAIN
2012

Communist Party of Ireland
43 East Essex Street
Dublin 2

Communist Party of Britain
23 Coombe Road
London CR0 1BD

www.communistpartyofireland.ie
www.communist-party.org.uk

ISBN 978-0-904618-55-6

Cover design based on the poster by Kevin Squires.
Connolly image by Robert Ballagh.

INTRODUCTION

GARETH MURPHY

YOU are very welcome to this year's James Connolly Memorial lecture, ninety-six years after the execution of Ireland's great working-class leader and Marxist intellectual by the forces of British imperialism.

This year's guest speaker is Robert Griffiths, the general secretary of the Communist Party of Britain. Robert lives in Cardiff and has been active for many years in the Welsh language and cultural movements and appears regularly on Welsh radio and television. He is the author of numerous books and pamphlets dealing with Welsh labour history and political theory. His work *Was Gramsci a Euro-Communist?* was recently republished. Robert will speak today under the title "Nationalities, nations, and imperialist globalisation."

A hundred years ago, before the outbreak of the great inter-imperialist conflict of 1914–1918, Connolly understood imperialism as a global system of economic, political, cultural and ultimately social control that divided the world between classes and between dominant countries and dominated countries.

For Connolly, imperialism was not just military occupation or the direct political rule of powerful states over weak ones but instead he correctly saw it as the capitalist system developed to such a degree, and in such an uneven manner, that left peoples all over the world oppressed by a foreign ruling class, with domestic complicity. It was this more complete understanding by Connolly that enabled him to see what many of his contemporary radical nationalists couldn't, namely that

> if you remove the English army to-morrow and hoist the green flag over Dublin Castle, unless you set about the organisation of the Socialist Republic your efforts would be in vain.
> England would still rule you. She would rule you through her capitalists, through her landlords, through her financiers, through the whole array of commercial and individualist institutions . . .

Connolly came to this insightful viewpoint not just as an advanced nationalist but as a socialist and, more importantly, a Marxist. On the explanatory power of Marxism, Connolly said:

Without this key to the meaning of events, this clue to unravel the actions of "great men" Irish history is but a welter of unrelated facts, a hopeless chaos of sporadic outbreaks, treacheries, intrigues, massacres, murders and purposeless warfare. With this key all things become understandable and traceable to their primary origin; without this key the lost opportunities of Ireland seem such as to bring a blush to the cheek of the Irish Worker; with this key Irish history is as a lamp to his feet in the stormy paths of to-day.

Connolly understood imperialism in the same vein as his contemporary Lenin. And Lenin's critique of capitalism, as it developed from Marx's time, remains the most complete and coherent outline of the system of monopoly capitalism—the highest and final stage of capitalism.

While the contradictions may have grown more acute and the tendencies stronger, Lenin's basic definition of imperialism still helps explain contemporary events. While recognising the limitations of concise definitions, Lenin outlined imperialism as the stage of capitalist development when

(1) the concentration of production and capital has developed to such a high stage that it has created monopolies which play a decisive role in economic life; (2) the merging of bank capital with industrial capital, and the creation, on the basis of this "finance capital," of a financial oligarchy; (3) the export of capital as distinguished from the export of commodities acquires exceptional importance; (4) the formation of international monopolist capitalist associations which share the world among themselves, and (5) the territorial division of the whole world among the biggest capitalist powers is completed. Imperialism is capitalism at that stage of development at which the dominance of monopolies and finance capital is established; in which the export of capital has acquired pronounced importance; in which the division of the world among the international trusts has begun, in which the division of all territories of the globe among the biggest capitalist powers has been completed.

Lenin, correctly, saw imperialism as capitalism developed to its monopoly stage, where competitive laws, as outlined by both Smith and Marx, no longer defined the progress of capitalism but monopoly growth, rivalry and contradiction defined the world and its division.

Contrast that with how Karl Kautsky, a contemporary of both Connolly and Lenin but one who betrayed the working-class cause of socialism for chauvinistic social democracy, defined imperialism.

Imperialism is a product of highly developed industrial capitalism. It consists in the striving of every industrial capitalist nation to bring under its control or to annex all large areas of *agrarian* territory, irrespective of what nations inhabit it.

Kautsky, incorrectly, limited his definition of imperialism to a policy by big countries of seizing land. Unfortunately, it is Kautsky's understanding that appears to hold sway in the broader left today, and also amongst some republicans. Imperialism has been disconnected from capitalism and is seen only as resource wars or aggressive military action to secure geo-political interests.

This narrow and limited view has very real political consequences today. It has led to a misunderstanding of what the EU is. Many see the EU merely as a grouping of capitalist countries. Yet the same people might claim the US is imperialist because it occupies and invades countries. This is incorrect and misunderstands the nature of imperialism today.

The Communist Party defines the EU as an imperialist bloc, because it is the political representation of the growth and development of big European monopoly finance capital. It, more clearly than ever today, works in their interests to divide and conquer both its internal and external peoples.

Understanding imperialism in the sense of the development of capitalism also helps us understand why there is a core and periphery within the EU and globally. The uneven development of capitalism amidst the merger of capitals and growth of monopolies left some capitalist countries capitalist but not necessarily imperialist.

So take Ireland—capitalist, no doubt, but one whose capitalist development was shaped by more powerful and dominant capital than our own. Consequently Ireland, while part of the imperialist system, is still subject to imperialism. And if anyone doubts this just remember Connolly's quote and look at the distorting and subjecting impact that capital flows from Germany, France and Britain have had over our economy in the last two decades, and now look at the capital that is being sucked out of the country back to those same countries.

This is also reflected in the continuous flow of capital out of this state, which will be institutionalised and given a legal framework if the two treaties are adopted. This is nothing more than a structured transfer of wealth from the Irish people to monopolies in the imperialist EU.

This is why it is still relevant to talk about national liberation and sovereignty as necessary steps towards socialism in Ireland, what is nominally, partially at least, a free and independent state. Likewise the Bolivarian revolutions in Latin America see the struggle for socialism as part of the struggle for sovereignty, and vice versa.

Those on the left who see capitalism and imperialism as separate abandon the struggle for sovereignty, national liberation, and transformation. They see imperialism only as relevant to the Six Counties and not the island as a whole or, worse, distort Marxism to such a degree that they justify the existence of the Six-County sectarian state and wallow in a swamp of "gas and water socialism," as Connolly called it.

Sadly, the abandonment of national liberation, the struggle for national democratic control and sovereignty by many big left-wing movements and forces has handed "nationalism" over to right-wing and fascist forces and allows them to present patriotism in its narrow chauvinistic sense. As in the past, fascism is the last line of defence for finance capital, for the system itself.

Today we see the growth of right-wing movements within the working class across Europe and still left forces failing to grapple with the nature of imperialism and liberation struggles within imperialism.

Someone, thankfully, that has not fallen for that folly is today's speaker, and I would now like to hand the microphone over to Rob Griffiths.

Thank you.

NATIONALITIES, NATIONS, AND IMPERIALIST GLOBALISATION

ROBERT GRIFFITHS

Cymrodyr, cyfeillion,

Ar gyfer Comiwnyddion, i'r mwyafrif o Farcswyr ac i lawer o sosialwyr, yr arwyddair traddodiadol sy'n llywodraethu ein hagwedd ni tuag at y cwestiwn cenedlaethol yw hwn: "Mae gan bob cenedl yr hawl i benderfynu ei dyfodol ei hun."

Dylai pob genedl fod yn rydd i ddewis bywyd gwleidyddol ar wahân, annibynnol, gyda'i gwladwriaeth sofranaidd ei hun fel y mynno hi.

Comrades, friends,

For Communists, most Marxists and many socialists, the paramount principle determining our approach to the national question has traditionally been summed up in the slogan: "The right of nations to self-determination."

All nations must be free to choose a separate, independent political existence, with a sovereign state of their own.

This was the principle adopted at the 1896 London Congress of socialist and trade union organisations, elaborated by Stalin for the Russian Bolsheviks in his articles *Marxism and the National Question* in 1913, and subsequently defended by Lenin against Karl Kautsky, Rosa Luxemburg, the Jewish Workers' Bund and the so-called "Austro-Marxists."

This principle was enunciated as capitalism was entering its final and highest stage, that of imperialism—the era of imperialist wars, anti-colonial revolts, and socialist revolution. More than a hundred years later, how has it stood the test of time, not to say real life? Should it still serve as our paramount guiding principle in relation to the national question?

After all, it is apparently a principle or slogan used by the imperialist powers to attack, weaken and divide states that obstruct imperialist interests and so defy imperialist hegemony.

- The "national rights" of the Slovenians, Croats, Bosnians and Kosovars were supported by Britain, Germany, the US and NATO to break up Yugoslavia and facilitate Western imperialism's economic, political and military drive eastwards.
- The "national rights" of the Chechens, Georgian Ossetians and others have been invoked to justify the division and destabilisation of Russia—a continuation, it could be argued, of the process that broke up the Soviet Union.
- The "national rights" of the Kurds have been used to justify NATO involvement in Iraq and—who can be sure—may be invoked again as part of the case for military intervention in Iran.
- The "national rights" of the Tibetans and of the Uygurs in Xinjiang Province (or "East Turkmenistan," as the separatists would have it) are trumpeted today to discredit and undermine a united, sovereign China.

Is not the right of nations to self-determination, therefore, a hostage to reaction—an abstract principle, or an empty, impractical slogan, one which ties our hands and opens the door for imperialist intervention and counter-revolution?

Should we not abandon it, and judge each national question purely on its merits, from the perspective of the political class struggle? Where autonomy, devolution, federalism or independence would benefit the working class and the struggle for socialism, it should be granted; where it weakens the working class and assists imperialism, it should be denied.

Such a pragmatic approach would, in my view, repeat past errors and actually play into the hands of imperialism. It would deepen divisions within the working class rather than help to overcome them. And it would strengthen tendencies towards opportunism and revisionism within the Communist and left-wing movement. It would be an approach based on a misunderstanding of the principle of "the Right of Nations to Self-Determination" and how it should be applied.

Marx, Engels, and the "principle of nationalities"

The past error to which I will primarily refer is that committed by Marx and Engels in the middle of the nineteenth century.

In that era of bourgeois revolution against absolutism and feudalism, when the capitalist class and its intelligentsia fought for political power against the landlords, financiers, monarchs and emperors in Europe, Marx and Engels rightly sided with the bourgeoisie and urged the emergent proletariat to do likewise.

But they noted that numerous small nationalities, such as the Scottish Gaels, the Bretons in France, and the royalist Basques, were what Engels, in the furrow of Hegel, called "relics of a nation," "residual fragments of peoples" who were "fanatical standard-bearers of counter-revolution."[1] Their territories were bastions of economic, social and political backwardness.

In the great revolutionary upsurge of 1847–48, on the promise of national autonomy (a limited form of self-government) and with the backing of Tsarist Russia, the Czechs, Croats, Slovenians and Ukrainians had sided with their own oppressors (the Habsburg monarchy) to crush the revolts of the Polish and Hungarian nationalists and the democrats of Vienna. Engels vowed that "for this cowardly, base betrayal of the revolution we shall at some time take a bloody revenge against the Slavs."[2] He insisted that "apart from the Poles, the Russians and at most the Turkish Slavs, no Slav people has a future, for the simple reason that all the other Slavs lack the primary historical, geographical, political and industrial conditions for independence and viability."[3]

Emperor Louis Napoléon of France, on the other hand, championed the "Principle of Nationalities," whereby all national peoples without their own state should be entitled to form one, to declare their independence, and—for example in the case of the French minorities in Belgium and Switzerland—to amalgamate their territory with that of their motherland. The Prussian, Austrian and Russian empires likewise embraced this "Principle of Nationalities," advocating it enthusiastically for rival empires while always finding it impractical to operate themselves.

Engels, on the contrary, argued that this principle was a Russian concoction (Louis Napoléon lacking the brains to have thought it up himself). Its aim was to justify the division and occupation of Poland and to stir up the Serbs, Croats, Ukrainians, Slovaks, Czechs and the "other remnants of bygone Slavonian peoples" in Turkey, Hungary, and Germany. Even as he wrote this in 1849, Russian agents were using the Principle of Nationalities to incite those "nomadic savages" (as Engels described them), the Lapplanders in northern Norway and Sweden, to set up an independent Finnish state (which, it was intended, would be dependent on Russia).[4]

Thus Marx and Engels opposed this "principle" because it was, in their eyes, a tool of reactionary intrigue (which indeed it was). The principle also meant, for instance, that the Romanians, who—according to Engels—"never had a history, nor the energy required to have one," were supposedly of equal importance with the Italians, with their two thousand years of history and their "unimpaired national vitality."[5] Indeed Italy was at that very time, 1866, demonstrating its vitality in an epic struggle for national unification.

Marx and Engels counterposed to the Principle of Nationalities what the latter called the "right of the great European nations to separate and independent existence."[6] Some of those nations had already exercised that right (notably England and France), while others, such as the Poles, Germans, Italians, and Hungarians, were struggling against imperial rule to do so. The "remnants of peoples," on the other hand, had shown no such energy and could therefore claim no such right to national self-determination. They would never become nations and embark on their own path of independent capitalist and democratic development: instead, civilisation would be imposed upon them by the great historic nations.

With incredulity, for instance, Engels noted that, according to the Principle of Nationalities, "the Welsh and the Manxmen, if they desired it, would have an equal right to independent political existence, absurd though it would be, with the English."[7]

This was the position he had elaborated for the International Working Men's Association, at Marx's request, in a series of articles in 1866 under the title "What have the working classes to do with Poland?" It was a harmful, potentially disastrous, approach. It cut across the slogan of *The Manifesto of the Communist Party* —"Workers of all lands, unite!"—and undermined the credibility of the First International's appeals for international working-class solidarity.

In particular, this standpoint detracted from their ideological struggle against great-nation chauvinism among the workers of the big and oppressor countries, enabling the German socialist leaders Karl Kautsky and Eduard Bernstein later to develop their case for a supposedly benign and civilising imperialism. It also assisted nationalists in the small and oppressed nations to portray the democratic and working-class movement as hostile to national aspirations, and provided more space for the imperialist powers to pose as the true defenders of the rights of small nations (as some went on to do in the Great Imperialist War of 1914–18).

Marx and Engels had, in effect, devised a Darwinian law of national survival of the fittest and applied it statically in a particular era of capitalist development: nationalities that had not achieved statehood by the 1860s, and were not even struggling for it, would never achieve it; they would remain marginal until their dissolution into one of the great historic nations. Such a prognosis is understandable, given the times through which Marx and Engels were living. How long could any nationality survive as a semi-feudal outpost in societies being transformed by the phenomenal productive forces of capitalism (forces, moreover, commanded by the national bourgeoisie of each historic nation, striving for and utilising state power)?

One legacy of this approach on the left has been to over-emphasise the possible transience of nations and, in particular, nationalities— even though many of the latter have so far survived two historical epochs without a national state of their own.

Yet even that wrong prognosis of Marx and Engels need not have ruled out the possibility of formulating a comprehensive policy on the national question for the working-class movement, as part of its democratic programme. They did not do so, perhaps fearing that even national demands short of independence would stimulate reactionary nationalism among what they regarded, almost by definition, as historically reactionary nationalities.

In my view, Marx and Engels had underestimated the capacity of capitalist development to transform the economic, social, cultural and political life—indeed, the social class structure—of even some of the smallest, most marginal and most traditional of nationalities and thereby compel a recomposition of their nationality and national consciousness on a new class basis.

Uneven economic and political development

The approach fashioned by Engels and Marx between the late 1840s and 1866 was quickly proved wrong by the flow of events, more specifically by the dynamics of the uneven development of capitalism, economically and politically. Before the close of the nineteenth century, capitalist development had accelerated hugely in many hitherto backward regions of Europe. Some nationally distinct areas —especially those with or near sizeable mineral fields—began to generate a locally based if not wholly indigenous bourgeoisie who commanded a distinct and at least partly autonomous market. An industrial working class could not but be formed in this process, along with an intelligentsia and other intermediate strata. In some places this new economic market and social class structure incorporated and reconstituted what had been a feudal nationality, with a native capitalist class or petit-bourgeois intelligentsia now redefining and directing it, culturally and politically.

Among some small or previously submerged nationalities, national movements arose on this new basis, demanding statehood or, at the very least, some of the national institutions and powers associated with statehood. Nationalities became nations as the accelerated development of their productive forces created an economic basis and a social superstructure that both transformed and reinvigorated national characteristics and national consciousness, rather than overwhelming and dissolving them.

Other small nationalities, of course, were either bypassed by this surge in capitalist development, or it occurred in conditions which restricted the emergence of a native capitalist class and intelligentsia, or militated against them identifying their interests with the foundation of a national movement, national institutions, or an independent state of their own. In other words, rapid economic development can, in certain conditions, serve to integrate a nationally distinct area and assimilate its people more fully into the dominant state and national identity. Some nationalities fail, through under-development or through rapid development of an unfavourable kind, to transform themselves into nations and thus face extinction as nationally distinct peoples. Is it pessimism, defeatism or realism to see this as the inevitable or likely future of, say, the Cornish and Breton nationalities? And what, for example, of the Manx people, whose national-cultural characteristics have all but disappeared and whose statehood exists primarily to serve the interests of an offshore *rentier* and British capitalist class?

Thankfully, Marx and Engels abandoned much of their approach to the national question within a short period of time, particularly under the impact of the national struggles in India and Ireland (although as late as 1885 Engels was dismissing the Serbs, Bulgarians, Greeks and "other rapacious riff-raff" as "miserable remnants of what once were nations").[8]

Having praised the civilising benefits of British rule in India in the 1850s, Marx turned into one of the most trenchant and implacable critics of the British Raj. From 1867 he supported the full separation of Ireland from England. Alongside Engels, his later researches revealed the extent to which a less-developed and what he had hitherto regarded as an under-civilised nationality could nonetheless have a rich history of its own—something they both discovered in their study of the early societies, laws and literatures of Ireland and Wales.

The condition of Ireland, especially in the eighteenth and nineteenth centuries, and its impact on the working class in England, impressed upon Marx and Engels the need to overcome national antagonisms between workers on a principled basis. This, in turn, meant approaching the national question in a precise, correct way. The national aspirations of oppressed peoples should be supported; the grip of reactionary colonialist and imperialist ideas on the working class of oppressor nations had to be combated, both without compromise. In his study of Indian and Irish history and development Marx also indicated a growing awareness of the connection between colonial and imperialist rule on the one side and under-development on the other.

The retreat of the revolutionary movement in Europe after the defeat of the Paris Commune in 1871, and the possibility of upheavals in the Russian Empire, also led Marx and Engels to pay more attention to the prospects of revolution outside Europe, to turn away from Eurocentric tendencies. Their deeper examination of the historical development of non-European societies produced a deeper appreciation of the role that could be played by anti-colonial movements. Marx even revised the French edition of *Capital* in 1875 to confine his model of "primitive accumulation" to western Europe.[9]

The Leninist approach

The spread of imperialism and of national and anti-colonial movements required a clear and agreed formulation on the national question from the advancing socialist movement; hence the London Congress resolution in 1896 for the full right of self-determination for all nations and for international working-class unity against capitalism, for socialism. In effect, the new slogan abolished the unhistorical distinction between "historic" and "unhistoric" nations.

But what, precisely, is a nation? Stalin elaborated and summarised a definition subsequently adopted by the Bolsheviks and the international Communist movement:

> A nation is an historically constituted, stable community of people, formed on the basis of a common language, territory, economic life and psychological make-up manifested in a common culture.[10]

This is still a workable starting point for defining a nation, although it needs to be understood in all its parts and their interconnections, and in its totality—all of which are subject to the constancy of change. But, in my view, this definition is itself inadequate and incomplete. As it stands, it draws no distinction between a nation and a nationality.

I am not arguing for resurrecting the theory of "non-historic" and "historic nations," not least because recent history has demonstrated how a nationality can become a nation. But I think there is a qualitative difference between the two—between, say, the Bretons or the Cornish and the peoples of the Irish or French nations. It revolves around the factor that is absent from Stalin's definition, namely the existence of national institutions—which reflect and reinforce the other characteristics of a nation—or of a substantial national movement in favour of creating such institutions, up to or including independence. Of course, dialectics teach us that reinforcing the existence of a national characteristic does not necessarily mean perpetuating it in its current form. It could involve, for example, adding a new or revived common language to an existing one, or replacing one kind of common economic life with another.

A nation possesses national institutions or a substantial national movement in addition to the other characteristics delineated by Stalin, whereas a nationality may not. Stalin's formulation on its own, it seems to me, defines a nationality that clearly has the potential to achieve nationhood, to become a nation which possesses a substantial national movement or national institutions and so has the right to independence.

But there are also, I would argue, nationalities that lack or have lost the prerequisites—the basis, the potential—to achieve independence. They have some if not all of the characteristics of a nation, but these are too few, too incomplete or too precarious to offer any significant prospect of advancing to nationhood. That might change with a major shift in objective conditions, obviously. At the risk of causing offence, I would place the Frisian people of the Netherlands (and northern Germany), the Lapps of Scandinavia and the Armenians of Turkey in this category.

Then there are distinct groups of people who may share a common ethnic origin, religion, language, territory or outlook but who are a minority within a wider nation, or derive from a parent nationality that is constituted elsewhere, perhaps as a nation. Again, no legitimate claim can be made for such a people to have the right of national self-determination, to declare separation from the wider nation and so cut across the latter's superior right to national unity and independence.

In my view, the Ulster unionist, loyalist and Protestant community falls within this category. It does not constitute a nation, which is not to say that its distinctive national origins, religious affiliations, cultural identity and so on are not worthy of recognition and accommodation. The Kosovo Albanians are a national group, but they are—or were—a minority within Serbia, whose territory they inhabited alongside an integral part of the Serbian population. Their claim to separation was specious, although it has been enforced by the Western imperialist powers through NATO.

All of this not withstanding, Stalin's definition of a nation was the basis on which Lenin developed a more systematic and comprehensive Marxist approach to the national question.

Firstly, Lenin insisted upon the absolute right of nations to self-determination, which could only be meaningfully understood to be the right to political separation and an independent political existence.

Of course, having the right to do something does not necessarily mean that it is wise to *exercise* that right in a given set of circumstances. Advocating the *right* to divorce, as Lenin pointed out, is not the same as urging every married couple to get divorced.[11] Whether Communists support national independence in any particular case should be assessed from the standpoint of revolutionary progress. Will separation advance the political class struggle, nationally and internationally? If not, revolutionaries should oppose the demand while upholding the right of the nation concerned to achieve it without undue obstruction should its people so wish.

Secondly, in his polemical battles against those who opposed or relegated the right to national self-determination, Lenin broadened the Communist and working-class movement's approach to the national question. His policy embraced nationalities and national minorities as well as established "nations." Thus, for instance, where a nationality forms a territorial majority it should exercise administrative autonomy (which today we might call devolution), whether or not it possesses or should exercise the right to full independence. All nationalities and national minorities—as well as nations—in a multinational state must have the right to use their own native language, receive education in it, and learn their own history at school. There should be no privileges or special status for any nation, nationality, or language.[12]

Thirdly, nations should as a matter of course exercise a degree of political and administrative autonomy together with the right to secede (as Finland did from Soviet Russia in 1918). In fact, faced with the problem of Great Russian chauvinism implicit in Stalin's scheme for "autonomisation" for the smaller nations and nationalities, Lenin overcame his aversion to federalism and advocated it in 1922 as the most transparent and consistent way to guarantee constitutional equality between the nations of what became the Union of Soviet Socialist Republics.[13]

Fourthly, in the more developed capitalist countries at least, Lenin treated the national question as being, in essence, a matter of democratic rights and democracy. He urged the working class to lead the fight for national rights, as it should for all democratic demands, thereby educating itself, winning allies, and equipping itself more comprehensively to lead the struggle for socialist revolution. He did not believe that national rights, or the fight for them, should be postponed to the other side of socialist revolution, any more than should the struggle for other democratic rights and liberties. His derision for such an approach is summed up by his reference to it as "imperialist economism . . . a caricature of Marxism."[14]

Fifthly, Lenin quickly grasped the importance of supporting national revolutionary movements in the colonies, to combat super-exploitation and under-development in the colony itself and great-nation chauvinism among the workers of the colonising nation.

He had much else of interest and value to say on the national question. He emphasised the need to analyse the class composition of nations, nationalism, and so-called "national" cultures. He argued for Communists and workers to be united organisationally within a multinational state. He drew a clear distinction between the nationalism of an oppressor country and that of the oppressed, declaring the former to be far more reactionary. He identified the special duty of revolutionaries in oppressor countries to combat their own great-nation chauvinism and to uphold the national rights of others. And he identified the special duty in oppressed countries to uphold working-class internationalism.

Here was the kind of national policy that Marx and Engels had not developed, although Engels was groping towards it in his final years. Lenin also emphasised the far bigger dangers of denying national rights instead of granting them. To deny a nation its right to self-determination is, in effect, to uphold the oppression of that nation by another; more precisely, it is to surrender to the great-nation chauvinism peddled by the ruling class, to acquiesce in the ideological domination of the working class by the ruling class; likewise when it comes to denying the rights of nationalities and national minorities.

Certainly, denying national rights tends to increase rather than resolve national antagonisms. As we have seen in the recent past, withholding or withdrawing autonomy from the Kosovars and the Kurds intensified national feelings and provided a pretext for the imperialist powers to invade and dismember Serbia and Iraq.

The national question in Britain today

In *The State and Revolution,* Lenin noted that

> even in regard to Britain, where geographical conditions, a common language and the history of many centuries would seem to have "put an end" to the national question in the various small divisions of the country —even in regard to that country, Engels reckoned with the plain fact that the national question was not yet a thing of the past, and recognised in consequence that the establishment of a federal republic would be a "step forward."[15]

In fact Engels had referred to the two islands of Britain—he can only have meant the British Isles—being "peopled by four nations."[16]

Well, the national question is still not a thing of the past in Britain. We now have a National Assembly in Wales, with limited law-making powers but with little economic power and only a very limited remit to raise capital funds through borrowing. The Scottish Parliament has more extensive legislative powers and a circumscribed capacity to raise taxation. The SNP government in Edinburgh is pledged to hold a referendum on Scottish independence in 2014.

The position that the Communist Party of Britain, and its Scottish organisation, is likely take in the referendum is set out in the new edition of our programme, *Britain's Road to Socialism*. We are for substantial devolution of power from the highly centralised British state to the nations of Britain—including substantial economic and financial powers—as well as to the regions and localities. In particular, we want the Scottish and Welsh governments to have the power and resources to be able to intervene decisively in the economy of their countries, in the interests of workers and the people generally, challenging the monopolies and their unfree market as and when necessary. This is a vital part of our perspective for the exercise of popular sovereignty, for the people to enforce their interests over those of monopoly capital. And if that puts those governments, those peoples and those workers on a collision course with the EU, so be it.

We uphold the right of the Scottish people and their elected representatives to hold a referendum on the terms that they decide, and to achieve independence should that be the people's decision.

But we oppose the separation of Scotland or Wales in current conditions. Why? Because our assessment is that any benefits from independence would be outweighed by the disbenefits likely to arise from economic dislocation, an upsurge in competing nationalisms, and—above all—from the rupture of working-class and progressive unity built up by the peoples of Scotland, England and Wales through two centuries of struggle and solidarity.

Our assessment is that the unity of British monopoly capital would survive national separation largely intact, and would undoubtedly play off the separate states against each other as the labour and progressive movements are divided along national lines. These do not provide more favourable conditions for overthrowing state-monopoly capitalism, which is why our opposition to such a trajectory is revolutionary and strategic. It is not based on British unionism or nationalism. Indeed we do not believe that the left and the labour movement should have anything to do with the reactionary arguments that will be employed by British unionists and nationalists against Scottish independence.

Of course, for instance, the people of Scotland are as capable of governing their own country as the people of Switzerland or Swaziland. Higher levels of social-welfare spending in Scotland are not proof of English or British generosity: they are evidence of continuing central-government failure to challenge the consequences of capitalist monopoly power, of capitalist market anarchy, and capitalism's uneven economic development.

Nor are we interested in making or keeping Britain "stronger" in Europe or the world. Breaking up British imperialist power would be one of the most desirable results of breaking up the British state— except that it would not happen. The British capitalist class would retain its enormous economic and financial assets around the world (all of them beyond the reach of the Scottish state), Scotland would continue to be a dominion of the European Union and NATO, and in the short to medium term at least England would be a particularly aggressive, nuclear-armed force in international affairs, allied to the USA. Furthermore, the indications are that an SNP-led independent Scotland would engage in a "race to the bottom" with the rest of Britain in the field of corporate taxation.

The SNP and Plaid Cymru slogan of "Independence in Europe" is a cynical hoax on the people of those countries. There is no independence within the EU for minor nations, who will be subject to EU laws, treaties and institutions without any of the power to influence or determine them enjoyed by the major imperialist member-states.

That is why the Communist Party rejects both reactionary unionism and reactionary separatism. *Britain's Road to Socialism* makes clear our commitment to a united fight for a progressive, democratic federation of self-governing nations, with the national and British governments pursuing a left-wing programme of anti-monopoly policies, free of nuclear weapons and breaking with British imperialism, the EU, and NATO.[17]

The advance of devolution in Scotland and Wales has helped to raise the "English question" in recent years, in particular the arrangements that should be made in relation to England-only legislation. The Communist Party's view is that this would best be resolved by the House of Commons reconstituting itself whenever necessary as an

English parliament, with only the English MPs present when considering such measures. There is the option of turning a fully elected House of Lords to this purpose, but our policy is that the second chamber should be abolished altogether, and all MPs compelled to do a full-time job.

A longer-term constitutional settlement, based on the unity of the three nations of Britain combined with substantial powers of self-government for each, might take the form of a federal system with new structures that reflect their equal status.

We also believe that the distinctive cultural and social characteristics of Cornwall should be expressed through a directly elected Cornish Assembly, with powers that match local aspirations. The special "tax haven" status enjoyed by finance capital on the Isle of Man and the Channel Islands, which are run politically as semi-feudal fiefdoms, should be ended. The peoples of those islands should be democratically represented in the Westminster parliament, with their own democratic parliaments—Tynwald and the States—strengthened by proportional representation and economic powers like those proposed for Wales and Scotland.

Imperialist globalisation and the European Union

Communists propose extensive economic and financial powers for Wales and Scotland, so that their governments and parliaments can intervene effectively in relation to monopoly capital, in today's context of capitalist or imperialist "globalisation."

Our programme argues that counter-revolution and the dismantling of socialism in eastern Europe and the Soviet Union from the late 1980s opened up enormous opportunities for monopoly capital to seize control of resources, transport routes, utilities and markets in the former socialist countries and the Third World. The result has been a prolonged and continuing worldwide imperialist offensive to maximise monopoly profit through "neo-liberal" policies of privatisation, deregulation, intensified exploitation of labour, and the free movement of capital.

This imperialist "globalisation" is presented by its supporters and apologists as an inevitable economic process. However, from the outset it has been driven politically by the most powerful state-monopoly capitalisms, notably those of the US, Britain, and Germany, often acting through new or existing agencies, such as the

IMF, World Bank, the World Trade Organisation, and the General Agreement on Trade in Services.

Third World countries whose regimes are deemed to be obstructing imperialist globalisation have been demonised as "rogue" or "failed" states. They are accused of frustrating the will of the "international community" (which usually means the US and its allies). Consequently, sanctions and other destabilisation measures have culminated in military aggression against Iraq, Lebanon, Libya, Somalia, and Yugoslavia.

The bogus "war on terror" has been the cover for extending and deepening Western imperialism's military, political and economic influence across the "Greater Middle East" region, from North Africa to Pakistan, inflicting state terrorism on the peoples of Afghanistan and Iraq on a monstrous scale. China is almost completely surrounded by imperialist military alliances and bases while forgoing any bases of its own on foreign territory.

Another major casualty of imperialist globalisation is the progress that had been made in resolving national inequalities and conflicts within the former socialist states of central and eastern Europe and the Soviet Union, since at least the early 1950s. Yugoslavia has been torn apart by imperialist intrigue and national chauvinism and large parts of it colonised by German monopoly capital. Czechoslovakia has been split into two even more unequal halves, one of them occupied by German, French and British capital, even though both peoples have far more in common geographically, historically and linguistically than their differences.

Most of the former socialist countries have collapsed into the arms of the European Union, which itself has played a leading role in promoting globalisation, confirming the EU's character as an alliance led by the most powerful state-monopoly capitalisms. NATO has expanded eastwards across Europe to all the western borders of Russia.

In the EU, the drive to overcome internal contradictions and transform itself into an imperialist "United States of Europe" is integral to the imperialist globalisation project. This drive has further undermined national self-government and the right to self-determination. But while EU agencies such as the Commission, the European Court and the European Central Bank play important roles in this process, it should not be overlooked that the state-monopoly capitalisms of the major EU powers are commanding the process. It is not a case of the German, British or French states, or ruling classes, being compelled to submit to the European Union and its institutions. To a greater or lesser degree, they are the architects of this drive and are complicit in it.

The workers and peoples of EU member-states, on the other hand, face a struggle to withstand this drive and its effects on their jobs and living standards and on their employment, trade union, welfare and other democratic rights. They need to influence the use of state power at the member-state and national levels in order to do so. But this is not a national liberation struggle—certainly not in Britain—of an oppressed country against a foreign imperialism. To think so would be to downplay or ignore the role of the British ruling class, the big finance monopoly capitalists, in exploiting and oppressing people at home and elsewhere, and in promoting the EU itself.

Therefore, there is no material basis for a supposedly "progressive" or "left-wing" British, say, or French or Spanish or Portuguese or Greek nationalism. These are not oppressed nations but imperialist states of varying power, where the main enemy of the working class is the bourgeoisie at home.

Nationalism—whether British, Irish, Welsh, Scottish, French, or any other brand—is a bourgeois or petit-bourgeois ideology which elevates "the nation" above class, above class analysis, class solidarity, and working-class internationalism. Capitulation to nationalism of any kind sooner or later disarms the working class, heightens national antagonisms, and demobilises if not liquidates Communist and other working-class organisation.

The serious error on the other side of the EU question is, in my view, to underestimate or deny—in the name of some abstract "internationalism"—the national-democratic importance of the struggle to assert popular and national sovereignty. Challenging the fundamentally pro-monopoly capitalist EU institutions and treaties will be significantly more difficult in a United States of Europe, should it come about, even with much greater solidarity between the workers of different member-states (which itself may be more difficult to achieve in a deregulated, dog-eats-dog labour market). Of course in the new phase of imperialism that is "globalisation" it is clearly in the interests of workers to unite their labour movements in action across national and state boundaries, against the transnational corporations, the policies of the EU, the European Court, and the IMF, against further moves towards a militarist, imperialist United States of

Europe, and so on. Proletarian internationalism lags behind the international co-ordination of capitalist monopolies and their states.

Nonetheless, the basis of capitalist rule remains the nation-state (or, in Britain's case, the multinational state). The EU, NATO, the IMF and other international agencies designed to operate in imperialism's common interests were created by—and rest upon—the national state power exercised by the capitalist class in their respective countries. Without that state power, whether in the US, Germany, Britain, or France, those international agencies would tumble like a house of cards.

For socialists and Communists, therefore, our most profound internationalist duty remains to carry through socialist revolution in our own country. This is also, after all, the level at which working-class and progressive, democratic movements have struggled to develop their organisations, their political consciousness, and their democratic rights. For Communists and the working-class movement to neglect this arena in pursuit of some will o' the wisp "United Socialist States of Europe" or suchlike is to sacrifice the fundamental, permanent interests of the working class in favour of a mirage. It would represent opportunism of a potentially very damaging kind.

Imperialist globalisation has already demonstrated its willingness and ability to trample upon national rights and sovereignty. At the same time it purports to embrace the rights of small nations and nationalities when and where it suits imperialist interests to do so—echoes indeed of the first Great Imperialist War.

This should not be the cause for socialists and Communists to abandon national rights. As recent election results in France and Greece have confirmed, if the forces of the left do not pick up the banner of popular and national sovereignty the right-wing nationalists and fascists will move in to do so.

The glimmer of a socialist future

Stalin drew a fertile distinction between the "capitalist nation" and the nation as it would develop under socialism. The "socialist nation" would be re-established on a different economic and social basis; its culture and political life would be filled with new class and democratic content; relations between its own nationalities and with other nations would be imbued with a spirit of equality, peace, and international solidarity—not based on annexation, exploitation, and the threat of war.[18]

The experience of socialist construction in the Soviet Union, Yugoslavia and Czechoslovakia—despite grave errors in this and other fields—provided a glimpse of the future "socialist nation." For relatively long periods, old national antagonisms were held in check and even eroded; whole nationalities were given political, cultural and linguistic rights and enabled to develop a modern industrial base; new, socialist "national" or multinational identities began to emerge (Soviet, Yugoslav, Czechoslovak) on the basis of formal equality between nations and nationalities, even if inequalities were not wholly eliminated in practice.

It is already evident that monopoly capitalism—imperialism—in the twenty-first century stifles the right of nations to self-determination, undermines economic and political sovereignty, and erodes the cultural and linguistic distinctiveness of all but the most powerful nations. To be a socialist and an internationalist increasingly means to defend national and popular sovereignty; to be a democrat and a patriot increasingly means to be a socialist and an internationalist. Incidentally, Lenin had no difficulty describing himself as a Russian patriot, enjoying and celebrating everything in Russia's history, culture and identity that was uplifting, progressive and in revolt against ignorance and oppression.[19]

But in fighting the democratic battles of the present, Lenin also looked to the future, when he wrote:

All nations will arrive at socialism—this is inevitable, but all will do so in not exactly the same way, each will contribute something of its own to some form of democracy, to some variety of the dictatorship of the proletariat ... There is nothing more primitive from the viewpoint of theory, or more ridiculous from that of practice, than to paint, "in the name of historical materialism," this aspect of the future in a monotonous grey.[20]

Heddiw, gymaint ag erioed, mae safbwynt athronyddol Marcsiaeth-Leniniaeth yn cyfuno'r cwestiwn cenedlaethol a rhyngenedlaetholdeb ar yr unig sail y gall sicrhau datblygu rhydd i bob cenedl, i bob cenedligrwydd, ac i bobl y byd yn gyffredinol—ar sail y frwydr ddosbarth, wleidyddol, yn erbyn cyfalafiaeth ac imperialiaeth, ac o blaid sosialaeth a chomiwnyddiaeth.

Today, as much as ever, the Marxist-Leninist world view synthesises the national question and internationalism on the only basis that can ensure the free development of every nation and nationality, and of humanity as a whole—on the basis of the political class struggle against capitalism and imperialism, for socialism and communism.

NOTES

1. Frederick Engels, "The Magyar struggle" (1849), *Marx and Engels Collected Works*, vol. 8, p. 234–235.
2. Frederick Engels, "Democratic Pan-Slavism" (1849), *Marx and Engels Collected Works*, vol. 8, p. 374.
3. Frederick Engels, "Democratic Pan-Slavism" (1849), *Marx and Engels Collected Works*, vol. 8, p. 367.
4. Frederick Engels, "What have the working classes to do with Poland?" (1866), *Marx and Engels Collected Works*, vol. 20, p. 157.
5. Frederick Engels, "What have the working classes to do with Poland?" (1866), *Marx and Engels Collected Works*, vol. 20, p. 157.
6. Frederick Engels, "What have the working classes to do with Poland?" (1866), *Marx and Engels Collected Works*, vol. 20, p. 157.
7. Frederick Engels, "What have the working classes to do with Poland?" (1866), *Marx and Engels Collected Works*, vol. 20, p. 157.
8. Frederick Engels, Letter to August Bebel (17 November 1885), *Marx and Engels Collected Works*, vol. 47, p. 353.
9. Karl Marx, Drafts of the letter to Vera Zasulich (1881), *Marx and Engels Collected Works*, vol. 24, p. 346.
10. J. V. Stalin, *Marxism and the National Question* (1913), *Collected Works*, vol. 2, p. 307.
11. V. I. Lenin, "The National Programme of the R.S.D.L.P." (1913), *Collected Works*, vol. 19, p. 543; "A caricature of Marxism and imperialist economism" (1916), *Collected Works*, vol. 23, p.72.
12. See, for example, V. I. Lenin, "The nationality of pupils in Russian schools" (1913), *Collected Works*, vol. 19, p. 533, and "Critical remarks on the national question" (1913), *Collected Works*, vol. 20, p. 44.
13. See, for example, V. I. Lenin, "The question of nationalities or 'autonomisation'" (1922), *Collected Works*, vol. 36, p. 605–611, and "On the establishment of the U.S.S.R." (1922), *Collected Works*, vol. 22, p. 421–423.
14. V. I. Lenin, "A caricature of Marxism and imperialist economism" (1916), *Collected Works*, vol. 23, p. 28–76.
15. V. I. Lenin, *The State and Revolution* (1916), *Collected Works*, vol. 25, p. 447.
16. Frederick Engels, "A critique of the draft programme of 1891," *Marx and Engels Collected Works*, vol. 27, p. 228.
17. Communist Party of Britain, *Britain's Road to Socialism* (2011).
18. J. V. Stalin, "The national question and Leninism" (1929), *Collected Works*, vol. 11, p. 353–354.
19. V. I. Lenin, "On the national pride of the Great Russians" (1914), *Collected Works*, vol. 21, p. 102–106.
20. V. I. Lenin, "A caricature of Marxism and imperialist economism" (1916), *Collected Works*, vol. 23, p. 69–70.